The *Agnes,* the *Clara May* and the *Traly*

Three Westcountry Ketches with a little History

Charmian Astbury

Published by:
Sappho Publications
43 North Street, Northam, Bideford
North Devon, EX39 1DH

British Library Cataloguing-in-Publication Data.
A catalogue record for this book is available
from the British Library.

ISBN 978-0-9539640-3-1
Printed in Great Britain by
Arthur H. Stockwell Ltd.
Torrs Park   Ilfracombe
Devon

Contents and Illustrations

Foreword

A Little History

The *Agnes*

The *Clara May*

The *Traly*

Endpiece

Acknowledgements

Foreword

This is the third in my series of small maritime histories of South West Britain. It has been an absolute delight to have had the privilege of personal correspondence and the one-to-one conversations with those who worked on these old ketches, as well as to have had access to their photographs, documents and individual bits and pieces that have not yet reached the locality museums and their archives.

The locality museums have been wonderful. The mainly volunteer museum staff have been more than helpful as they themselves get to grips with the continuous arrival of new archive material, (which, as the years pass, happily continues to arrive), current re-organisations and refurbishments, and in one instance, administrative material lost in river flooding. My local library, as always, remains my major route to the publications, both old and new, that I wish to access.

As is the case with my two earlier books in this series, I like to just note the issues about accuracy of information, particularly dates and sources. There will always some blurring of information, blurred, among other things, by the constant re-organisations and subsequent re-naming of just about everything. So, a museum that was once familiar by the town name may now be identified by a certain generic name. Collections of historic papers and photographs may have been moved, quite logically, towards the generic name and so on. I have a simple rule of thumb: should my source be a known and respected one, then that is the one I use. With dates I use the date used by the majority of sources, which is subject to its own weaknesses in that such may be based on blurred information anyway. I am always delighted to hear from any reader who has more accurate information about dates and sources. In fact, this small book got going because of such a communication. And, unsurprisingly, more than one source will hold the same information, thus sources and individuals are acknowledged separately. Errors in the use of the material are the author's own.

The history of these islands of ours is becoming less and less visible as the years pass and this is very true of the history of South West Maritime Britain. The recording of history is always vulnerable to the influences of the time. What I have been able to do, indeed privileged to do, with all my small books is to have been able talk to and correspond with some of those who experienced, and recall, working aboard the last of the Westcountry ketches. History is what happened. The narrative of this little history attempts to hold onto the narrative of what happened for a particular part of South West Maritime Britain during a particular span of years. And what happened can only draw on what went before. Thus there is a very brief look at a thousand years of 'what went before' the ketches appeared on the scene to introduce 'ketches *Agnes*, *Clara May* and *Traly*'.

1a. Draughtsman sketch of a typical Bude ketch, *Clara May*, from 'The Story of Budehaven', Rennie Bere, 1977

75.5 feet long and 19.5 feet wide; main masts 8 feet from the keelson with a 30 foot top mast and mizzen of 38 feet. She carried three jibs, a stay-sail and a gaff-topsail Her gross tonnage was 72.56 and net tonnage 69.61 Her dead weight cargo capacity was approximately 115 tons. English oak, English and American pine, pitch pine and yellow pine were all used in her construction

1b. *Clara May* dimensions, from 'West Country Coasting Ketches', WJ Slade and Basil Greenhill, 1978

A Little History

Three ketches, the *Agnes,* the *Clara May* and the *Traly,* are the focus for this little history of South West Maritime Britain. Why these three ketches? With five or six hundred Westcountry ketches out and about in all weathers doggedly plying their trade, especially during the nineteenth century, why just three and why these three?

Well, for a whole variety of reasons these three ketches today, in 2007, are still within living memory. There are one or two other ketches out there able lay claim to this attribute and some of these are still sailing. However, the *Agnes,* the *Clara May* and the *Traly* were each drawn to my attention following the publication of my two earlier books in this series, 'The Story of the *Dido C*' and 'The Ketch *Ceres* 1811-1936'. And this is because the men who had known or had sailed aboard ketches *Agnes, Clara May* and *Traly,* as working vessels some fifty years or more ago now, having read what I written about the *Dido C* and the *Ceres,* contacted me to talk about their own particular ketch vividly recalled with real affection some fifty years on.

These conversations have been wonderful for me as I gradually collected, sorted and re-arranged the jig-saw bits and pieces of maritime history that came my way. But, I still needed to know just what had been so significant about the ketches in general that they should be remembered at all, let alone in such detail and with such affection. Slowly and steadily a maritime history of the coasts and ports of South West Britain began to emerge from the spoken word, the carefully produced fifty-year-old and faded newspaper cuttings, the old photographs and invoices, scraps of this and that including a bolt from a 'friendly fire' shot as well as a dockyard document, with the heading 'top secret', long supposed destroyed.

It was what the ketches did and how they experienced what they did within their varied lives and times that was to prove the key to these recollections. From the late eighteenth century until the mid-twentieth century the ketches had been the trading vessels of their time. Under sail they had been a, if not the, central part of coastal everyday life for some hundred and fifty to two hundred years. These Westcountry ketches sailed to ports and estuaries far and near on a more-or-less daily basis dependent upon the tides, the weather and the wars - of which there were many. Sometimes these small vessels could be gone for weeks or months at a time depending on what they were doing and where they were going. And some never returned.

The ketches carried goods and commodities here there and everywhere reachable by sea, river and estuary. In so doing they had provided an essential service to all concerned. Fuel, (coal, culm for lime-burning, wood); food, (flour, grain, root vegetables); fertilizer, (guano, slag, lime and limestone); building materials, (timber, bricks and stone); salt cod from the other side of the North Atlantic; household items – anything and everything that could be transported, traded and landed at the harbours or run onto the shores and beaches, was transported and traded.

The ketches also had to carry food for those who sailed them. Before their diesel engines were installed, which was quite late on in their history, this would have been little more than salt cod, flour, tea, and water with possibly some potatoes and dripping. With the advent of the small semi-diesel engine towards the end of the nineteenth century the ketches became increasingly nimble in getting about. Their supplies began to feature perishable foods such as milk, fresh bread, meat, eggs and similar. Alcohol in some form or other, probably rum, would appear to have been a foregone conclusion on board used both for comfort and medicine. And there was sometimes a dog on board, who would also need his rations. Any dog would have been a much loved member of the crew, so much so that there are recorded instances of a formally mourned death of the on-board dog in the traditional sea-farer's manner, including the mourning bands painted around the outside of the vessel.

****

The ketches were small, some of them very small, wooden sailing vessels of well below one hundred tons in weight able to run onto the shores and beaches of the coasts and estuaries of South and West Britain. The ketches were family owned and, more often than not, family built. The ownership was within a system of shares supported by a mutual insurance framework. The financial returns were at best modest and often non-existent. However, as well as the provision of the much needed goods to their communities, the ketches were also able to provide some paid employment for the men and the boys. And also the women at times, though the women were more likely to assist with the work of unloading and, most of all, with the reading, writing and numeric skills needed for the accounting requirements. The coastal communities not only worked their seaborne trade but also lived and breathed it.

This robust self sufficiency would have been, in part at least, the legacy of the coastal and maritime communities own history: their survival was very much their own affair and always had been. The distant centres of government, money and power, even had such expressed an interest, were far too far away to be able to deal with the constant threat of starvation, of privation and disease, of pirates stealing goods and slavers stealing people. It has to be remembered that people, animals and goods have always been the currency used by all when there was little else to trade.

It is difficult nowadays to be able to have an awareness of just how alone and isolated were those sea-faring communities of South West Britain, situated days away by land from both their local and national governments. Their 'country' was the sea whose vast stretches of bordering coastline provided them with their trade and trading partners. The coastlines of England, Ireland, Scotland and Wales, Scandinavia, Iceland, Europe and the Mediterranean, Africa and North America were all part of this maritime trading world, as were the ever present threats of piracy, untimely death and loss. During the virtually continuous wars there was the additional threat from privateers. These privately owned vessels provided fighting power for their own governments and were far from averse to intercepting non-combatant traders, such as the ketches, for their own personal gain. The ketch *Good Intent*, built at Plymouth in 1790, was one such. She was captured by a French privateer six years after she had been built and is pictured here moored some hundred years later at Bridgewater, the Somerset brick trading port, around 1896.

2. The ketch *Good Intent* moored at Bridgewater c1896

The privateers were individually owned vessels of any country. They operated under licence from the government of that country to capture what they could of men, goods and vessels belonging to the enemy. The enemy changed so frequently that the local seamen, or for that matter anyone else, had little hope of knowing whose side they were on when challenged or attacked. The Spanish, French, American, Dutch and others (as well as ourselves viewed from the opposing sides), were all within the frame at one time of another. Wholly vulnerable, the seamen could have been murdered on capture, put on board other vessels as booty along with their cargo, sold to slavers, marooned anywhere they could be abandoned - Lundy was much favoured for this cruelty. There was little difference between a pirate ship and a privateer as far as an individual seaman was concerned. No wonder the indigenous sea-faring communities of the various warring factions tended to look out for each other rather than bother whose side who was on.

****

Without doubt there was always ever present danger and hardship in a trading life at sea, but it was the sea-borne trade that provided the sea-farers and the maritime communities with their livelihood. However, the South West Peninsular itself had always been of political and strategic importance to the rulers of Britain as well as to their counterparts on the Continent and elsewhere. The granite island of Lundy, off the North Devon coast some miles into the Atlantic from the Bristol Channel, has a long, violent and, perhaps not surprisingly given its strategically important position in the South West, a well documented history with still extant records dating from the 12th century. So although little interest was shown in the wellbeing of the people of the South West, over the centuries a great deal of time, money and energy was invested by all interested parties into the control of Lundy. The Kings of Britain, those of France and Spain, the Dutch, the North Africans, not to mention the marauders and pirates from anywhere and everywhere, all held temporary control, seemingly anything from a few days to centuries. Lundy was useful to one and all both as a raiders' stronghold and as a dumping ground for unwanted captives.

There is strong evidence to suggest that the first member of the Marisco family, whose name still adorns the Lundy tavern and whose family controlled Lundy for the longest period of time, was an illegitimate son of Henry I of England. Henry I must have felt that he had solved not only the security of his kingdom but the safety of his son in one astute political decision. This situation may go some way to explaining why, instead of being thankful that there was a good man and true holding Lundy for the Crown, the legitimate line of English Kings from 1155 onwards persecuted the Marisco family until they had managed to execute in 1242 Sir William Marisco, the then family head, in the usual horrible manner of the day, after which any meaningful Crown or government control of Lundy seriously lost ground to general marauding and piracy.

Once the Crown's interest in the Marisco family had well and truly gone matters became progressively worse. During the centuries that followed, the Island of Lundy was, to use a modern phrase, 'up for grabs'.

As the 1400s progressed, Ilfracombe, although providing a harbour considered to be a refuge for shipping from both storms and attack, was promoting its own piracy of one sort or another as were most other ports and havens in the South West and not just Ilfracombe. Again, one has to bear in mind that the coastal inhabitants had little or nothing to help them survive, let alone live, beyond limpets, crabs, a little trade and a little fishing. When in 1463 a Basque vessel carrying cloth under safe conduct to Bristol, took shelter from the weather in Ilfracombe harbour, it was the local landowner, one Lord Fitz-Warren, who plundered

The Marisco Family and Lundy

Mid 1100s: Henry I: the first Marisco on Lundy was probably this king's illegitimate son

1155: Henry II demanded the return of Lundy to the Crown

1160: Henry II attempted to grant Lundy to the Templars without success

1194: Henry II fined Marisco for non-surrender of Lundy

1199: King John, recently king, confirms gift of Lundy to the Templars with again no outcome

1216: King John now has Marisco against him and siding with the Scots and French

1217: Henry III on the throne grants amnesty to the Mariscos with regard to Lundy

1235: Henry III: Marisco implicated in political murder returns to Lundy with family in haste and turns to piracy in the Bristol Channel for survival

1242: Henry III: Sir William Marisco executed in London following betrayal on Lundy

1242/45: Henry III: island remains important to kings so Lundy castle and fortifications completed

1281: and the Mariscos are still claiming Lundy

1321: Edward II and Lundy is back with the Crown

1326: Edward II trying to seek Lundy and safety is captured and murdered in Berkeley Castle

1326 until 1390: Lundy is held for the Crown by the Earl of Salisbury and various others over the years all of whom raised the money and negotiated the finances for the running of the island, including one Stephen de Marisco

3. Some dates: the Marisco Family and Lundy

her. Cloth would have been not only a valuable but an essential commodity to all in the locality and Fitz-Warren was having it. Small boats would also row out to plunder vessels at anchor in the harbour. Usable items to trade or use, such as food, rope, sail cloth, tools and similar would be taken and those on board thankful to still have their lives.

At the end of the fifteenth century, in 1492, the ownership of the strategically positioned island of Lundy, having passed from one powerful individual to another, once again reverted to the Crown, following the death by drowning of Lundy's then holder, the Duke of Clarence, in his butt of malmsey…..

****

The next century fared little better in terms of piracy world wide as well as that experienced around the coasts of South West Britain, with Lundy invariably the focus of interest. Recalling the success of Sir Francis Drake in waylaying the Spanish treasure ships from South America it is hardly surprising that the Spanish were always trying to capture Lundy as a base from which to attack England. Indeed, captured Spanish pilotage notes of the time mention Lundy as a good refuge, and Spanish State Papers record that Lundy was likely to be used by those plotting against the Crown. The Spanish were on Lundy for a time in 1597.

Earlier in the century, however, the local communities had started to take matters into their own hands. In the 1540s there is mention of the fishermen of Clovelly launching a successful attack against the pirates then on Lundy, capturing them and burning their boats. Following what must have been a helpful clear out to the local hopefuls, the local pirates once more used Lundy as a raiding base; John Piers of Padstow in the 1560s, Robert Hicks of Saltash in the 1570s, John Challice in the 1580s to name but a few. In 1587 Barnstaple launched a successful attack against the pirates on Lundy at a cost of five shillings and five pence, a huge cost to the authorities at the time. The Barnstaple based authorities would not launch another attack until empowered by the Crown to have the title to any spoils. This was granted in 1610 with the expedition finally launched in 1612, (successfully), after two years spent in arguing over the division of the hoped for spoils. In the meantime Elizabeth 1st had come to the end of her long reign and James 1st and 6th was on the throne. And the piracy and raids continued to terrorise the South and West coasts of Britain until finally the feared North African Corsair slavers, the Sale pirates, were able to raise their loathed dark green and black flag on Lundy in 1626.

****

The Sale pirates, the North African Corsairs, ravaged and plundered quite specifically and most successfully Europe, Britain, Ireland, Scandinavia, Iceland and North America from their North African ports for some three hundred years until the beginning of the nineteenth century. In excess of one million white and mainly Christian European men, women and children were abducted and sold into slavery during these centuries, an estimated three hundred thousand of them from the coasts of Great Britain, which is roughly a thousand a year for three hundred years. One of the more spectacular raids in the Westcountry saw a whole church congregation abducted from Mounts Bay in Cornwall. Most of these unfortunate people were never heard of again. They perished in dreadful circumstances, some of them latterly in the building of the planned three hundred miles of palaces of the North African Sultan Moulay Ismail. Dying where they stood, their remains were shovelled into the lime with which they were working.

Successive governments appeared powerless to prevent the raids or the misery and suffering that followed, probably because of the numerous wars in which all of them were involved, mainly fighting each other. In the British Isles these slave raids were not only perpetrated upon the isolated coastal communities but also upon major cities such as Plymouth, Bristol, Cardiff, Dublin, Hull and London. There was no meaningful defence anywhere. Petition after petition went to the Crown, even the slave widows travelling from the Westcountry to London to petition the king, but there was little if any help, either financial or political. Charles 1st, though, did send an undercover agent who had some success in buying back some hundreds of the thousands enslaved before the double-dealing being practiced by all involved brought this to an end. It is perhaps worthy of note here to realise that it was around this time that *Rule Britannia* was published in which appears the telling line 'Britons never, never, never, shall be slaves'.....

Thus it remained just far too easy for the unprotected to be snatched from their beds, from their shores, from their streets as well as from their small sailing ships. Their subsequent deaths mattered not at all to the Sale raiders who had captured them, they merely captured others. Slavery was a lucrative business, the men selling for thirty-five pounds a head, (the women and children captured were highly prized), in the North African slave markets – and all witnessed by the various ambassadors and churchmen of the day who not only ministered to the needs of those so sold but also recorded how they felt for them in the unfortunate circumstances in which they found themselves........

It was not until 1816, during a quieter period with regard to wars, that a naval expedition was launched, headed by one Sir Edward Pellow, (a later kinsman of the Cornish eleven year old Thomas Pellow who survived over twenty years as a slave in the palaces of the Sultan Moulay Ismail), which succeeded in destroying Algiers and the fifty strong slaver's fleet at anchor there. At long last were Britain, Europe and Scandinavia free of this particular terror. The slavers continued to conduct their vile trade elsewhere, most notoriously between Africa and North America and in the West Indies, but, for the most part, but not completely, Europe had freed itself.

****

So, back to the first years of the nineteenth century in South West Britain and to the life and times of the Westcountry ketches. One particular Westcountry ketch, the long-lived *Ceres*, can now be found recorded in the first Lloyds Lists for 1814. Originally built to bring fruit from Spain to England, the *Ceres* had been commandeered at the beginning of her very long life to run supplies to Wellington's troops fighting in the Napoleonic wars on the Portuguese mainland. The *Ceres* had been built in 1811. Later on the effects of the American War of Independence would also be experienced as American privateers took over from those of France, albeit briefly, sailing the trade routes and seaways.

Tough but successful years lay ahead for the trade of the Westcountry ketches. The coming century was to prove, in spite of the wars, the weather, competition and social change, good for trade. A case in point is the ketch *Ceres*. The *Ceres* traded for one hundred and twenty-five years, from 1811 to 1936, bringing an estimated forty thousand pounds worth of business into her home port of Bude in Cornwall. The greater, and latter, part of her life, a full eighty years of it, was within the ownership and care of the Bude family of sea captains and merchants, the Pethericks. The Bude ketch *Agnes,* built in 1835, was another vessel with a long life ahead of her. However, as is always the way in the affairs of men and women, as fast as one lot of threats and challenges are resolved, others just as overwhelming appear to fill the spaces.

****

The ketches were built of timber which was more often than not harvested from the local hedgerows and woods. The timber, in particular that which would have included the massive oaks needed for the naval and larger merchant ships, would have been harvested much nearer to the major dockyards and ports. Shipbuilding in general, however, had developed wherever there was sea-going expertise and large volumes of timber were imported to meet this requirement.

On the shores of North Devon's River Torridge alone, between the years 1800 to 1808, one hundred and seven merchant ships and seven war ships had been built. So the supply of timber for shipbuilding in Britain was essential and the demand never ending.

The Baltic ports provided the timber routes from Scandinavia and Russia. Now, Napoleon had successfully organised a blockade of the Baltic ports in the November of 1806 and by July 1807 he had negotiated the support of Russia, Prussia and Denmark for this blockade. The British Navy still controlled the Baltic Sea, and indeed largely controlled the timber harvest in Britain, but the situation was desperate. In 1806, when the price of a load of timber had been fifteen shillings, Russia had sent to Britain 297 loads of timber, Prussia 6,000 and Norway 1,400. In 1808 some loads were still getting through the blockade, but the respective number of these loads had fallen to 19, 27, and 69. By 1809 the price of a load of timber had risen from fifteen shillings to sixteen pounds. The British finance houses, in order to safeguard the huge investment needed to support the supply of timber, imposed prohibitive duties on any imported timber. These duties were not completely revoked until 1860, some forty years after they had first been imposed, such was the power and influence of the timber lobby, by which time Napoleon and his blockades had long ceased to be an issue. And by 1860 North Devon's timber and shipbuilding connections with North America had become very well established indeed.

Napoleon had hoped to be allowed to reside in England following his defeat at the Battle of Trafalgar and capture some years later. In fact he had enjoyed a certain celebrity status while held onboard the *Bellerophon* while she was moored at Plymouth during the summer of 1815. Napoleon and a small entourage were exiled to the remote South Atlantic Island of

St. Helena in October that same year where he died some five and a half years later.

However, the continuing joint influence of Napoleon's blockades and the duties imposed by the timber lobby during the first half of the nineteenth century proved to be an overwhelmingly serious issue to the shipbuilding communities. A steady supply of affordable timber remained essential to the shipbuilding requirements of Britain. The shipbuilders of North Devon's Torridgeside, within the first year of Napoleon's blockade, had found their solution.

The timber merchants and shipbuilders of North Devon, faced with the end of everything they knew and had worked for, recognised that the answer lay thirty days sailing away across the North Atlantic. The North Atlantic had been crossed by sailing vessels time out of mind for millennia. The ketches themselves had traded along parts of the eastern seaboard of North America, frequently returning with salt cod. It was known, therefore, that there were vast forests there that could be meaningfully harvested. And these mariners knew how to equip their small sailing vessels in order to survive for a long time at sea.

So, it was to Prince Edward Island, situated off the eastern shores of Canada, that the timber merchants and shipbuilders set sail from the ports of Appledore and Bideford in North Devon, a weather dependent crossing under sail of some thirty days, to harvest the timber needed to build their vessels. On 31st October 1812 there came the first direct consignment of timber into the Port of Bideford from Prince Edward Island, probably delivered to Thomas Burnard, shipbuilder of Northam and Bideford. Furthermore, what these capable men were able to develop was a viable commercial structure of building the timber shells of their vessels on Prince Edward Island and sailing these back to Bideford and Appledore, with additional timber on board, to be completed.

It was the shipbuilder Thomas Chanter of Northam himself, having bought out Thomas Burnard in 1816, (and having put his own shipwright William Ellis on the island to build the ship shells), who each summer set sail for Prince Edward Island from Bideford with the shipbuilding supplies needed. In 1827 he was put ashore on Prince Edward Island with the raw materials needed both for shipbuilding and the preservation of the winter's food. Three of the vessels built during those first early decades were the *Collina*, 1827; the *Calypso*, 1828; and the *Sappho*, 1829. It was the *Collina* that sailed from London in the summer of 1827 with groceries, household hardware and so forth for the stores of Port Hill and New Bideford on Prince Edward Island.

Four and a half tons of cordage, 15 tons of salt
20 barrels of tar, 5 barrels of pitch, 2 barrels of resin
5 casks of white lead, 10 sails, 3 anchors

---

4. Thomas Chanter's 1827 shipbuilding supplies from Bideford to Prince Edward Island

---

6,250 pounds of soap, 6,000 pounds of candles,
9 puncheons of rum
2 puncheons of brandy, 2 hogsheads of brandy,
9 hogsheads of genever
600 pounds of coffee, 37 tons of cordage as well as dry goods,
groceries, paint, hardware and similar

---

5. Thomas Chanter's 1827 household goods from London to Prince Edward Island

The actual harvesting and supply of timber was developed and handled by the Cornishman William Yeo, who settled on Prince Edward Island with his second wife and family. William Yeo's first wife, whose death was probably due to the hardship and starvation common to her time, is buried in Kilkhampton churchyard. However, in spite of the steady supply of good timber organized by William Yeo, Thomas Chanter had a great deal of trouble with his shipwright on Prince Edward Island.

The shipbuilding specification had to be quite detailed on the vessels to be completed at Bideford and Appledore because of the duty payable on the timber. But there was a lot wrong with the vessels being delivered for finishing and Thomas Chanter's correspondence on the subject becomes more and more irate. The brig *Sappho*, built in 1829, is a case in point. In 1830, a year or so before the *Agnes* was built at Bude, the *Sappho* was moored at Bideford. Thomas Chanter states in his letter of the time to his shipbuilder on the other side of the Atlantic, that round the bows of the *Sappho*, the plank was 'so shook' that 'everyone at Bideford Quay noticed it'. The comments of those gathered on Bideford quayside were so strongly to the point that the order was given to turn the *Sappho* round! Furthermore *Sappho's* top gallant boards had to be taken down and there were no openings or hinges in her bulwarks and waist.

There were similar problems with his other vessels built around the same time, but in spite of all this, that same year there was an advertisement in the North Devon Journal dated 24th June 1830, stating that the vessels *Collina*, *Calypso*, *Sappho* and *Euphemia* were 'conveniently fitted up for families and will take out passengers to Prince Edward Island, Cape Breton, Nova Scotia or New Brunswick'. Passengers were carried from Falmouth, Plymouth and Cardiff as well as from Bideford. The advertised fare was twenty-five pounds for cabin passengers and three pounds for an ordinary passage. People were so desperate to leave these shores that the first exodus of settlers, many of whom were in comfortable circumstances, left that summer of 1830.

The timber harvested from the other side of the North Atlantic was, in the main, softwood, such as pine and tamarack. Elm was used for the keels. These softwood built vessels, mainly three and four-masted barques, had a lifespan of some twenty years or so. The shipbuilding of Canada's Maritime Provinces developed to meet this continuous need. For instance, towards the end of the century in 1878, the Maritime Provinces of New Brunswick, Nova Scotia and Prince Edward Island built well over four and a half thousand vessels. The Westcountry ketches, which were built on this side of the Atlantic in North Devon and North Cornwall, were built of hardwood and so were able to last longer, barring war and disaster. Some ketches survived into their second hundred years. The Bude ketch *Ceres*, built at Salcombe in 1811, sailed until she foundered in 1936 off Baggy Point in North Devon. The *Agnes*, built at Bude in 1835, was similarly long lived, lasting until 1957, although controversy still remains as to whether or not she was the same vessel after her rebuilding in 1903.

****

So, turning now to the three ketches of this little history, the *Agnes*, built in 1835, the *Clara May*, built in 1891 and one of the early non-timber built ketches, the *Traly*, built in 1912. This little history of these three ketches, vessels that served their communities well, illustrates the diverse lives and times of all the small vessels serving the Westcountry coastal trade. In so doing a remarkable strand of the maritime history of South West Britain comes into the 21st Century in a very real way.

Agnes: 1835 to 1957

6. The ketch *Agnes*, outward bound from Bude, August 1936

Official Number: 105246
Built 1835, Bude, Builder: Stapleton
Rebuilt: 1903/4, Bude, Builder: Rudland Bros (ongoing query as to whether same vessel)
Bude Owners: O Davey, NH Tregaskes, Peter Herbert
Braunton Owners: Billie Mitchell, H Clarke, F Wright
Last and out-of-trade owner: Alistair Barr
Names: *Lady Acland*, (1835), *Margaret Frances*, (1904), *Agnes*, (1910)

Net registered tons: 54
Port of registry: Bideford

Main trade coal from Welsh ports and Lydney, Gloucestershire, to Cornish ports
Main trade during WW2 flour and cattle feed to Barnstaple
40hp semi-diesel engine 1920s
50hp diesel engine installed 1948
Sold 'out of trade' 1956
Wrecked in a hurricane, West Indies, 1957

7. The *Agnes*: her key dates, owners, registration and main trade

24

The *Agnes* was built at the Bude shipyard of Robert Stapleton probably in 1835. She was first built as the *Lady Acland* for the Bude merchant, Mr Oliver Davey. On his death in 1897 both the *Lady Acland* along with her sister ketch, the *Sir Thomas Acland*, were bought by Mr Edward Rudland, merchant of Holsworthy who died in 1901. It was in 1901 that the *Lady Acland* was lengthened by his sons, the brothers Arthur and Edward Rudland, in the Bude shipyard and renamed the *Margaret Frances* after their niece. The additional fifteen feet increased her cargo capacity by thirty tons, from seventy-five to one hundred and five tons. Her additional weight does not appear to have been recorded officially, for she remains at 54 tons for all of her life.

In 1910 the brothers sold the *Margaret Frances* to Captain NH Tregaskes of Bude who renamed her *Agnes*, after his ketch of that name lost in the great blizzard of March 9th 1891. This was the blizzard that, following a morning forecast of mild north-easterlies of force four, by mid-day had turned into an easterly hurricane that raged for two days and nights devastating the counties of Devon and Cornwall. Recovery from the damage and destruction took the best part of a generation or more. There were at least seventy vessels lost with their crews. Trains and villages were cut off by deep and drifting snow. Large numbers of farm animals were lost, as was wild life and woodland. One resident of Bude today, a local author, recalls that his grandfather used to tell him how he had helped *his* father round up what ponies and sheep they could reach from the nearby moorland and bring them down to shelter and food.

Following the death of Captain Tregaskes in 1913 the *Agnes* passed to his son Percy who sold her some years later, in 1918, to a Liverpool firm. One reason given for the sale out of local coastal waters was said to be because of the enemy submarine menace during the First World War: another was the continuing financial burden of her rebuilding.

8. The *Agnes* coming into Bude from Lydney with coal, probably for the gas works, June 1st 1910, the hobblers waiting nearby to give assistance

9. The *Agnes* moored at Lower Wharf, Bude, goods train for cargo behind, 1939

10. The *Agnes,* Porth Clais, St David's, the Old Roman Quay
in the background, 1952

11. The *Agnes*, possibly the last vessel ever to come up in the coastal
trade to Wadebridge Quay, swinging at her moorings there in 1955

Six years later the *Agnes* returned to the local coastal trade, mainly carrying coal from Wales to North Devon and Cornwall, having been bought in 1924 by a Braunton consortium, the captains William (Billie) Mitchell and Harry Clarke, (18 shares each) and Dr Frederick Wright, (28 shares). Captain Billie Mitchell sailed the *Agnes* in the coastal trade for over thirty years until his retirement from the sea when she was bought in 1955 by Captain Peter Herbert of Bude, and returned to her former haunts.

****

In 1931, coming up to her first century, Billie Mitchell Jnr, as a three year old and the son of her then captain, was first taken aboard his father's ketch, the *Agnes*. He was aboard her every summer from that date on until he left school at the age of fifteen to join his father as crew. Billie Mitchell worked aboard the *Agnes* for nearly fourteen years with his father until 1955 when the *Agnes* was sold. Making a living from the coastal trade had become more and more difficult. Captain Billie Mitchell sold the *Agnes* on his retirement to Captain Peter Herbert, at which point his son, Billie joined his uncle Fred Mitchell in the sand and gravel dredger business.

Captain Peter Herbert sailed the *Agnes* in the Bristol and coastal trade for a few more years before selling her out of trade to Alistair Barr of Oban in Scotland. This last owner of the *Agnes*, a former merchant seaman, raised a crew of twelve men and six women, who each paid one hundred and sixty pounds to join him on the hoped for voyage to New Zealand. The North Devon Journal of 10th April 1957 carried a positive account of the plans for her, but there was a feeling locally that the *Agnes* was possibly inappropriately rigged for such a voyage and that her crew were not sufficiently experienced, (and the accommodation somewhat cramped). Percy Tregaskes, responded with a letter to the press in May 1957, the month

28

History of the Agnes

Sir,—As the second owner of the Agnes, I have been interested in reading about her preparation for her forthcoming voyage to Australia.

Before being lengthened she was the Lady Acland, owned by Mr. Oliver Davy, who sold his business as merchant to a Mr. Rudland, which included the Lady Acland. He was advised to have her lengthened to carry about 100 tons instead of 70 tons. When she was on the stocks he was surprised as to costs incurred, so asked my father, Mr. N. H. Tregaskes, to take her over, which he did, and had the work completed, fitted her out, and renamed her the Agnes after the first Agnes, built in 1878, which he owned and was lost in the Great Blizzard of 1891.

My father ran her until 1913, when he died and left her to me. I then had her chartered to run cargoes of coal from Newport to Clonakilty, in Southern Ireland, and back to Bristol with barytes and oats. She continued these voyages during the First World War up to 1917, when, in the month of November, while running to Clonakilty in a south-easterly gale, she had to enter Kinsale harbour for shelter, where she dragged her two anchors and went on the rocks, knocking the keel out of her, and other damage.

She was discharged and patched up sufficiently to sail to Appledore, where a new keel was put into her and repairs done, in three weeks, and she was ready for sea again and continued her voyages to Ireland. On one passage she passed over the spot where the Lusitania was sunk the day after it happened.

About that time I was warned about the submarine menace, when a Liverpool firm who wanted her asked if I would sell her, which I did. From then she changed hands a few times until Mr. Herbert sold her for this voyage to Australia.

She is a strongly-built ship and a good sea boat. I made some voyages in her myself, and, with good luck, she should reach her destination safe and sound.

J. P. TREGASKES.
1, Bramble-hill, Bude, May 6.

12a. Letter to press from Percy Tregaskes, May 1957

The little Cornish ketch *Agnes* sailed from Appledore on May 6, bound for Las Palmas, and eventually Australia, via Panama, Tahiti, and Tonga. As reported last month, sailing was delayed until the ketch's life-saving equipment satisfied official requirements. On May 1 she left P. K. Harris and Sons' yard, where she had been completing fitting out, and berthed alongside the schooner *Kathleen & May* at Appledore quay. After self-inflating rafts and a new ship's boat had been supplied, clearance was given. When she eventually sailed, she had a crew of 19—10 men and 9 women—including a press photographer who will leave at Las Palmas. The master, Mr. Alistair Barr, one of the few on board with experience of sail, told reporters that he hoped to reach the Canaries in about 15 days.

12b *Sea Breezes* report June 1957

she actually left Appledore for Las Palmas, in which he sends his good wishes to the *Agnes* and her crew. A report of her May departure is to be found in the June 1957 issue of *Sea Breezes*, which also mentions the hoped for Australia destination, by way of the Panama Canal, Tahiti, Tonga and New Zealand. The *Agnes* made it as far as the West Indies where, during a hurricane off Barbados, she broke her moorings and was wrecked. There was no loss of life.

****

The financially viable trading years of the ketches started to disappear during the first years of the twentieth century hastened not only by the changing transport systems but also by the effects of the two World Wars. The commandeering of the Westcountry ketches for barrage balloon work during the Second World War destroyed many of these, by then, aging wooden sailing vessels. The still working ketches, being wooden, were also frequently used as decoy vessels to sail over the minefields of the South Western Approaches. Being blown out of the water by floating mines was one fate: another was being blown out of the water by enemy shipping for it was known that the ketches were being used as decoys. The ketch crews, in these latter instances, were usually allowed to abandon their vessels for their small rowing boats before this happened.

The massive changes in the economy, in transport, in social trends and similar that followed Second World War completed the demise of the ketches. Most of those that managed to survive the war were either abandoned along the tidal mud flats or sold out of trade in an effort to diversify and have some return on investment. This last was the fate not only of the *Agnes* but also of quite a number of others, including two Braunton ketches, the *Clara May* and the *Dido C*, neither of whom made it beyond the dreams of their last owners.

ROUTE-BARRY TO ILFRACOMBE, BARNSTAPLE, APPLEDORE
                        BIDEFORD, FREMINGTON.

Leave Barry Rds...........   INDEPENDENT SHIPS ONLY.

On leaving Barry Roads, all vessels are to signal their International Letters
to Nell's Point Signal Station.

            Navigation Lights are to be exhibited *North of* 51° 00 N   and Irish Sea.

WRECKS AND BUOYS-BARRY NO.18.

Fairway   51 22.18 N 03 10 24 W. Can Buoy Gr.Fl.(R) 2 ev.15 secs.
Eden Force.   51 25 00   03 15 12
Devonia.   51 22 40   03 14 50   Gn.Can Buoy Fl. Gn(2) ev.10 secs. 2 cables
                                                  137° from wreck.
Wythburn   51 22 34   03 15 07

Pass to the Eastward of Wreck Marking Buoy in Barry Roads in posn. 51° 22' 30" N.
03° 14' 42" W. Fl.Gn(2) ev.10 secs.and enter a   Channel 2 cables
in width at posn.51° 21' 06" N. 03° 14' 00" W. thence to (1) below.
The Southern edge of this Channel joins the Breaksea L.V. and the Middlesex Wk.Buoy.
The centre line of the Channel joins the following positions. Kee to starboard.

ILFRACOMBE.
(1) 51 20 40 N   03 17 45 W. 000° - 2 cables from Breaksea L.V.
(2) 51 24 00   03 57 42   227° - 4 cables from Scarweather L.V.
(3) 51 12 45   04 06 30

                    Channel 4 cables wide (1) to (2)
                       "   "   "   (2) to (3)

BARNSTAPLE, APPLEDORE, BIDEFORD AND FREMINGTON From (2) to (..) 51 16 00 N 04 04 00 W.
Thence follow the coast as closely as safe navigation permits but keeping outside
the 3 mile limit or anchoring during hours of darkness.
            entering by daylight. Vessels routed as above are permitted to be
under way during daylight hours only.

NOTES. 1. Barry Roads Anchorage   Ships must anchor between the meridians of Merkur
Buoy and 03.11 W.

        2. Prohibited Anchorage Anchorage is prohibited within the Compass Adjusting
Area, and also in an area enclosed by lines joining the following positions:-

                    Bendrick Rock.
                    51° 22' 43" N.   03° 14' 00" W.
wreck buoy in 51 22 30   03 14 38
                    Nell's point T.W.S.S.

3. All vessels approaching or at anchor in Barry Roads must keep a good lookout
for Signals made by the T.W.S.S. If a ship is unable to sail as ordered a
report must be made to the N.C.S.O. either by telephone or by signal through
the Port War Signal Station.

4. The utmost vigilence is necessary on the part of your A/A Guns' Crews at all times
whether the ship is at anchor or under way, in order that fire may be opened
instantly on low flying aircraft or on any aircraft which approaches within 1,500
yards unless it has been established beyond all doubt that the aircraft
concerned is friendly.

5. During an Air Raid, all ships at anchor in the Bristol Channel must keep a
sharp lookout for falling mines and report the bearing and estimated distance
of any which are seen to drop, indicating at the same time the exact position
of the ship.

6. Your Pilot should be shown such portions of your orders as concern him, and
all instructions in writing must be delivered to N.C.S.O. on arrival.

13. Secret WW2 navigation instructions issued to the *Agnes* on leaving Cardiff

The pre-war and wartime glimpses of the life and times of the *Agnes*, gained from Billie Mitchell's own recollections present a very real picture of the issues of the day. His stories, his collection of photographs, the old invoices from his father's day, and one simply stunning Second World War dockyard document that is headed ' Secret', each and all contribute to this lively look at her history.

Why any authority would head a document they wished to remain secret 'Secret' is beyond belief. When handed a selection of sixty-year-old yellowing papers of one sort or another by Billie Mitchell in the summer of 2005, the very first one that caught my eye was the one headed, in block capitals, 'secret'.

During the Second World War instructions were handed to the ketches, (and other independent shipping), from the Welsh ports before returning to their home ports. These instructions contained the secret navigation instructions for their route home. These were needed in order not only to avoid recent submerged or floating wreckage for that particular journey but also, should there be an air attack, that their route be known to their own side. The one illustrated here was from the Dock Office at Cardiff and lists the expected ports of call, buoys and navigation points for their route.

Included in the document are also exhortations for the 'utmost vigilance' to be observed, that any pilot should only have the information of immediate relevance to him and that the document should not fall into enemy hands. Captain Billie Mitchell would have gone to the Dock Office before leaving port in order to pay the harbour dues and to inform them whither he was bound. The Naval Control then issued him with the Sealed Letter that was to be opened once they were at sea. The document had to be handed to the appropriate authorities once the destination port had been reached. This one document from all the trading journeys of the *Agnes* alone has survived, probably mislaid under all the charts and other documents as she carefully made her way across the Bristol Channel before turning to hug the coast southwards towards her destination port. Local knowledge of the routes was what allowed the ketches to continue their sea-borne trading: there were no radios or telephones, let alone satellite navigation systems, in those days.

****

Their auxilliary engines, troublesome though they could be, allowed the ketches to keep close into the hazardous rock strewn coastline as they went about their various trading activities. However, having no radio contact presented a number of communication difficulties during wartime. The cargoes were generally sorted out by telegraph at their ports of call but communication between ports did come up with some unique problems. Much communication was by voice alone. Shouted one-to-one communication from the shore was possible once the engine was turned off. However, as the semi-diesel engines were notoriously tricky both to get going and to keep going this was not as easy as it might first appear.

The early semi-diesel engine was a large structure, with such a high and wide domed cylinder that a man could barely get his arms around it. The whole thing had to be warmed up before it could be started, first of all by a blow lamp for ten minutes and then by a heat bulb on the top of the engine for twenty minutes before the fly-wheel could be swung by hand. Furthermore, something in the order of a gallon of oil was required to start the engine. So, starting or restarting was quite an enterprise and there were frequent break-downs. Although they still journeyed under sail, being towed from the open sea to port was fairly commonplace. The recently restored *Kathleen and May*, (now moored at Bideford), following one such breakdown during the Second World War, towed the *Agnes* from the Nash just below Barry on the Welsh coast to the Bell buoy in Bideford Bay, North Devon.

H·WIDDOP & Co. Ltd.
Diesel Engine Builders

ESTABLISHED 1898

HEAD OFFICE & WORKS
GREENGATE
KEIGHLEY
ENGLAND

OUR REF.
JW/BG/

YOUR REF.

12th September 1950.

Capt.Wm.Mitchell,
M.V. "Agnes"
c/o Merchant Navy Club,
Avonmouth.

Dear Sir,

We have been requested by Captain
Harry Clarke to send you "One - New Oil
Pressure Gauge" and write you regarding wet
(oily) exhaust.

If your original pressure gauge is
faulty you may have been running with too high
a pressure. After fitting the new gauge adjust
to 6 lbs per sq.inch and see if this cures the
trouble.

If you are still troubled with excessive oil
in the exhaust (after fitting the new gauge and
setting the pressure to 6 lbs) the possible causes
are:-

1.)   Two much clearance in big end bearings.

2.)   Blow valves or pipes from crankpits choked.

3.)   Gudgeon Pins slack in piston holes.

14. 1950 letter, from Widdop & Co. of Keighley,
about the *Agnes'* 1948 installed engine

Communication was never easy, always remaining somewhat basic. Working with a difficult to start and restart engine added to the difficulties during wartime. There was one time that the *Agnes* was hailed by the coastguard, (who would have had access to the telegraph), shouting and waving his arms about, from the Valley of the Rocks on the Exmoor coast. The engine had to be switched off to enable his shouted message to be heard, telling them to proceed to Swansea and not to Barry. It took the full half hour to restart the engine before they could be on their way. And all that time at the mercy of the weather, the tides and the enemy. The relief once the new diesel engine was installed in 1948 was enormous,' you just pressed the button' and it started straight away. But even that had its moments as is shown by the letter of illustration 14.

Another time, the time when a friendly fire bolt from a tank exercise hit the *Agnes*, the communicated warning of danger ahead was just a red flag stuck in the hillside around the side of the headland that could not be seen on the approach to Ilfracombe. Apparently there was a practice involving tanks going up and down steep slopes while firing. The precipitous Exmoor coast hogbacks do not provide for a view from their landward slopes of small vessels hugging the coastline…..Billie Mitchell has the bolt which fell into the rigging that day, missing those on board and still hot when picked up from the deck. Friendly fire was a not uncommon hazard, wartime or peacetime. On one occasion the *Mary Eliezer*, a Braunton owned ketch built in Germany in 1904, (and photographed on 14th January 1998 while moored at Valletta, Malta), survived with a mattress stuffed in the hole after a practice torpedo had passed through her bows.

The scraps of paper and parts of invoices and similar that have survived, just as with the 'secret 'navigation instructions issued to the ketches, do bring to life the issues of the day. One that never failed to enrage Captain Billie Mitchell was the scrap of paper illustrated on page 38. This was a 1930s incident. On entering the

Bude Canal he needed an additional length of rope to moor at the quayside. The harbour master threw him a twenty foot length. When the manoeuvre was completed, taking in all some ten minutes the rope was handed back and a two shilling charge was levied. This was not only unexpected but an enormous cost at the time. The comparison with the cost of a ton of coal or the water taken on board shows this very clearly. Billie Mitchell's father insisted on having a signed receipt for his two shillings, illustrations 16. A comparison with some later costs, shown in illustrations 15 and 17, fully explains Captain Billie Mitchell's fury at the earlier two shilling levy.

Another occasion that angered Captain Mitchell on a later date was the charge for water demanded by the Bristol authorities. The on board supply of water was, needless to say essential. On 29th of October 1952 the Port of Bristol Authority charged Captain Billie Mitchell six shillings for the water supplied. Had this been taken on board at Bude he would have been charged one shilling. When he protested he was told 'take it or leave it'. There could only be one decision. The charge was paid and water was never again taken on at Bristol.

The *Agnes* experienced an interesting, active, well-loved and affectionately remembered life, whatever the debate about her age, whether in trade or out of trade, whether at work or at play. The ketch crews knew each other, more often than not were family members and enjoyed a comradeship that lasted throughout their lives and those of the following generations. In times of danger they were there for each other and competed determinedly when it came to seamanship or trade.

TELEGRAMS. "EXLUNCOLE, BIRMINGHAM."
TELEPHONES, CENTRAL 7408 (3 LINES).

LONDON, MANCHESTER, STOURBRIDGE, WOLVERHAMPTON ETC

REFERENCE
YOURS   OURS
            M/J

LUNT BROTHERS,
COLLIERY AGENTS.

Partners
E.A. LUNT.
A.H. LUNT.

TRADE **LUNT** MARK

Head Office:
No 13. Colmore Row,
Birmingham 3

25th. September 1941

W.Mitchell Esq.,
9,Station Road,
BRAUNTON,
North Devon.

Dear Sir,

        We are in receipt of your letter of the 24th inst.,
re freight on cargo of coal Port Talbot/Sharpness, 100 tons at
12/8.

        We understand from Mr.B.G.King of Bristol, our
Representative that the Schedule price is 10/3.per ton.

        We await to hear from you.

                        Yours faithfully,

15. 1941 letter to Captain Billie Mitchell concerning the cost of 100 tons
of coal

Received from Captain W. Chiddell

two shillings for use of

check rope in the locks.

E.B.Maynard

16. Receipt for the charge levied on ten minutes use of rope at Bude, mid 1930s

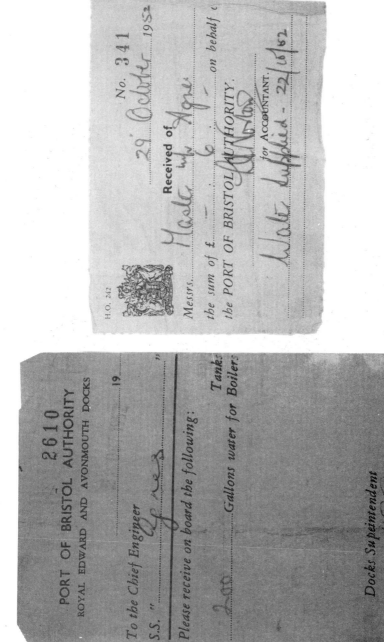

17. Receipts for water charge at Bristol 1952.

H.O. 242

No. 341

29 October 1952

Received of

Messrs. Haste w/o Agnes

the sum of £ — : 6 : — ... on behalf

the PORT OF BRISTOL AUTHORITY.

for ACCOUNTANT.

Water supplied - 22/10/52

2610

PORT OF BRISTOL AUTHORITY
ROYAL EDWARD AND AVONMOUTH DOCKS

19

To the Chief Engineer
S.S. " Agnes

Please receive on board the following:

Tanks

200 Gallons water for Boilers

Docks Superintendent

18. Sam Mitchell, Billie Mitchell and Len Baglow,
with the model of the *Result,* Braunton Museum, 2004

19. The *Agnes* unloading grain for Spillers Flour Mills, Roath Dock, Cardiff, c.1950s

The ketch *Clara May*: 1891 to 1957

20. The ketch *Clara May*, between Appledore and Instow, probably 1949/50

Official number: 99255
Built 1891, Millbay Dock, Plymouth
Builder: Watson & Fox
Bude Owner: JB Cornish 1920 -1923
Braunton Owners: A Parkhouse, H Clarke 1923 -1953, Mr Kent 1953-57, J Perkins 1957
Other Owners: J Merrifield, Feock; J Reed, Yeovil; T & J Hitchcock, Lavenham

Net registered tons: 69
Port of registry: Plymouth

50hp diesel engine fitted 1926
Main trade wheat, flour, grain and slag
Traded until 1953
Abandoned at Braunton Pill 1953, set alight 1957

21. *Clara May*, her key dates, owners, registration and main trade

In recent years Ray Harris, who had worked as the young crew, or in his own words as 'cook, boy and dogsbody' on the *Clara May*, for eighteen months, from 1949 to 1950, has enjoyed taking his family on holiday to Malta. In 2004, during an unexpected shower of rain while walking through the town of Bugibba there, shelter was sought at the nearest place, which turned out to be a bar and restaurant bearing the name 'Clara May'. Ray Harris just could not believe what he was seeing........

Inside the restaurant he discovered a good-sized and authentic model of the *Clara May* in a glass case. On the wall behind and above the model there was a framed copy of the 1949/50 photograph of the *Clara May* in the Torridge estuary between Appledore and Instow, (illustration 20). The restaurant's coloured glass window to the outside world was of a small sailing ship in full sail at sea with the words 'Clara May' curving above the stylised waves. Ray Harris knew full well that the *Clara May* never had traded to Malta, unlike the German built and, at one time Braunton owned *Mary Eliezer*, which may well have carried some cargoes to Malta. The *Mary Eliezer* was certainly in Malta during these first years of the twenty-first century. In fact, the Malta Times in 2004 carried a feature article about the *Mary Eliezer*.

Ray Harris was able to learn from the owner of the Clara May restaurant that the large framed photograph of the *Clara May* had been given to them by an unidentified lady from Braunton and that the model of the *Clara May* had come by way of Germany. Making accurate models of their ketches, as well as the painting of and, later, taking photographs of, their ketches was what the ketch crews did. Such pastimes were always far more of a homage to their small vessels than a hobby.

Illustration 24 shows Mr John Heard with his model of the *Clara May* that he presented to the Bude Historical & Folk Museum, now the Bude-Stratton Museum. This was when the

22. Ray Harris outside the Clara May restaurant, Malta, in 2004

23. Model of *Clara May* inside the Clara May restaurant, Malta.

24. John Heard with his model of the *Clara May* presented to
the Bude Historical & Folk Museum in 1976

museum first opened in June 1976 and even then well over twenty years after the demise of the *Clara May*.

25. *Clara May*, inward bound Newport to Bude
114 tons of coal onboard 31st August 1902

Ray Harris left school in July 1949 and joined the *Clara May* on the August Bank Holiday of that year. The *Clara May* was lying at Cardiff docks and to reach Cardiff from Ray's Braunton home was a bus ride to Ilfracombe followed by the Campbell's paddle steamer across the Bristol Channel to Cardiff. Captain Alfie Parkhouse of the *Clara May* came to Braunton to travel with Ray to this, his first job. The mate at that time was Jackie Bowden of Appledore. The very next day the *Clara May*, with her new full crew, sailed to Avonmouth to await a cargo.

The middle years of the twentieth century were those that presided over the end of the cargo trading days of the ketches. This meant that, by the time Ray Harris joined the *Clara May*, she and the other ketches still hoping to trade were by no means always busy or being worked. When the end-of-the-forties cargoes did arrive at Avonmouth they were, more often than not, of Canadian wheat. The fortunate ketch or ketches that had secured this cargo would move into position alongside the bulk grain carrier. The loading was simple. A chute from the carrier into the ketch hold and 130 tons of grain was delivered very speedily indeed! The task of the crew then was to lie flat on the grain so delivered and push it bodily into the corners of the hold. The only appropriate comment that can be made about such information is that those of us who were around at the time and are still going strong today would have eaten the bread milled from the grain so handled.....

The wheat was taken from Avonmouth to Cardiff where Spillers Flour Mills were situated. The old Spillers Flour Mills, now a modern day four-star hotel, were at Cardiff East Dock: the later Spillers Flour Mills were at Roath Dock, Cardiff and this is where the photograph of the *Agnes* delivering grain was taken, (see illustration 19). It is the Roath Dock Flour Mills with which the young Ray would have been familiar and it is these that have been totally demolished. Discharging the grain took about an hour for it was sucked up by a vacuum system and then it was back to Avonmouth to line up for another cargo.

In fair weather the *Clara May* could sail on the inner side of the large sandbank lying along the route. Chancy weather meant a much longer route around both this hazard and the lightship marking it, thus making for a longer journey and a possible missed cargo.

On a number of occasions the *Clara May*, and other small craft, would be tied up at the same time as the banana boats from the West Indies. From time to time a bunch of bananas, having been dropped overboard, probably deliberately during unloading, would float down to the ketches and would be fished out of the water by their crews and eaten there and then. Bananas at the time were still a somewhat rare post-war commodity and provided a much appreciated treat particularly for the ketch youngsters who had probably never seen a banana during their wartime childhoods, let alone eaten one.....

The quiet times also produced dangerous and difficult work for Ray in his employed role of 'boy'. One fine summer day, while sailing up the Bristol Channel, the captain sent him up in the bosun's chair to oil the mast with a bucket of linseed oil and a wad of cotton waste. Ray recalls, looking back on the experience, how 'the ship looked very small below me'! The re-rigging of the sails at Avonmouth, when manila was used instead of hemp, produced real problems in that manila swelled when wet whilst hemp didn't. Each time the mainsail was lowered, Ray had to climb the rigging in order to feed the halyards through the blocks.

The weather was judged for sailing as it occurred. In fine summer weather, and 1950 was a very good summer, the ketches would sail with the tide. In the 'dodgy' weather, 'we would walk out to the Mumbles beach to assess the sea conditions'. Come the winter it was a completely different situation and the *Clara May* had some really bad crossings. One night the goose neck on the mainsail broke and Ray was called on deck to help. All he could see was the mainsail crashing into the rigging, first one side and then the other. The mate, Bronco Ford, after a struggle by all involved, managed to lasso it and make it fast. Another night the bilge pump broke and they all had to spend the night manning the other pump to stay stable and afloat. Ray reached home exhausted and fell asleep on the sofa as soon as he arrived. Yet again he was under pressure from his family to 'pack it in'.

****

The transport of the cargo was how the living was made working the ketches and the competition was fierce as the crew were only paid by the trip. Life on board, therefore, could get somewhat tense. On one occasion during Ray Harris' time the *Clara May* was lying at Avonmouth for six weeks without a cargo. The young ketch crews were for the most part all former school friends. This provided the youngsters with company during those times, but for the older married men several weeks without pay was disastrous. The *Traly* was known to always have cargo and a berth onboard her was much sought after. The mate of the *Clara May* at the time Ray joined left soon after to take a berth on the *Traly*. He was replaced by another married man from Appledore, Bronco Ford, who insisted on being paid a retainer when there was no cargo, and he won the day.

The pay for Ray Harris at this time was £2.10s.0d a trip for a cargo of wheat, £1.10s 0d for a part load trip with oats and barley from Cardiff to Barnstaple and £4. 0s 0d a trip for the basic slag run. Three slag trips every two weeks provided real riches for a very young man. Slag, used as a soil improver for pasture land, was a potentially dangerous cargo, for, should the sea water get into the slag, the vessel became extremely unstable. The *Ceres* foundered off Baggy point in 1936 while carrying slag from Swansea to Bude after sea water got into her hold. Ray's family were very much against him staying with the *Clara May* while in the slag trade as the *Clara May* was known to be a 'bit leaky' and not in 'very good health' at the time. However, it was the summer of 1950 and the weather was very good indeed.

After loading grain, loading the slag was a new experience for Ray Harris. The slag, an industrial by-product akin to volcanic dust, was taken to the quayside by lorry in bags. A chute passed from the lorry to the ketch hold. One person loaded from the chute by catching the corner, or 'ear' of the bag and twisted the bag so that it landed exactly where intended in the ketch hold. Working from the centre of the hold, the bags were placed in rows across the hold with the 'ears' all pointing the same way. This made for both stability and easier unloading, when a crane and a chain loop would be used to get the bags out of the hold and onto the quayside.

Loading would take a couple of days and both the ship and the crew would get covered in the black dust. Wash time was a bucket of warm water with some soap in the forecastle, which also served as the eating and living quarters.

Much to the relief of Ray's family, the decision to 'pack it in' was soon taken out of the young Ray's hands. Ray had his last trip with the *Clara May* with a cargo to Fremington. Having berthed, the local engineer Walter Mills, who was aboard the nearby *Agnes*, was needed and brought over by young Billie Mitchell in the rowing boat. The engineer looked over the bulwarks into the engine room and gave it as his opinion that he had seen better sewing machines! However, he must have agreed to do something later, for the *Clara May* was unloaded. That Sunday, a gale sprang up and the *Clara May*, now unloaded and empty stove in her port side on the quay.

The *Clara May's* captain, Alfie Parkhouse, collected Ray from Braunton, probably in the rowing boat, and took him back to Fremington to help him sail the *Clara May* over to Appledore Dock for repair. Ray was offered the option of staying on dockyard wages or leaving. He left. Five months later he had joined the Royal Navy.

****

The final months of the *Clara May's* sixty-six years turned out to be very well publicised indeed as what took place during those final months was reported meticulously in the local press. The *Clara May* had, in effect, been abandoned at Braunton Pill in 1953 after having supposedly had a large amount of money spent on putting her in order by her then owner. There were local rumours of plans to sail her round the world 'trading in pepper and mother-of-pearl'. However, both her owner and the two men helping him with the work disappeared completely from the scene, one after the other, and 'the *Clara May* was left there.' A good three years later, in 1956, by which time the *Clara May* had eventually broken loose, Braunton Parish Council stepped in. She was causing damage to Vellator Quay and becoming a serious threat to the sewer pipes there, moving with every high tide and strong wind that blew, with the water pouring through her and finally partly blocking the outlet of the little river Caen where this went into Braunton Pill.

Braunton Parish Council consulted their solicitors. It was deemed that the owner had died and the vessel was handed over to local auctioneers, at which point the owner re-appeared...... only to then refuse the twenty pounds offered at auction! The Parish Council were becoming desperate, particularly in view of the threat of seasonal flooding from the Caen; 'It's not a rowing boat you know', the local press reported, gleefully noting *verbatim* the cut and thrust of Parish Council debate, 'it is no good burying your head in the sand about the job.'

Then something rather interesting happened. It was reported in the local press on 7th February 1957 that the *Clara May* had been sold privately to a Braunton man, who predicted that she would soon leave the mud of Vellator Quay to set sail for the Far East with a local crew to take on a cargo of pepper. The new owner was hopeful of sailing her, saying, 'other ketches are still sailing and I do not see why the *Clara May* should not. She will use her sails most of the time but will have an engine.' It was a substantial report under the heading 'Mystery Ship to sail for the Far East'. Somewhat surprisingly the national press picked up on the story, by which time, and carefully reported in the local press on February 13th, and within days of the earlier 7th February report, her owner had changed his mind.......

Both the BBC and the Ministry of Transport wrote to Braunton Parish Council about the *Clara May* report. 'Do they want it for television', asked the Chairman, to which question the Clerk to the Council replied, 'They called it a Tall Ship, but it is just a Tall Story.'

26. *Clara May*, Braunton Pill, August 1927

Whatever was taking place behind the press reports, and a number of conclusions may be inferred, it is certain fact that, on the evening of 20th July 1957, Braunton firemen answered a call to find the *Clara May* on fire. The fire had started in the cabin, pierced her deck but was contained. The episode was duly reported in the local press the next day.

27. *Clara May* moored at Bideford Quay, 1920

The *Traly*: 1912 to 1991

28. The *Traly* in the Avon Gorge, probably 1951

Official Number: 128846
Built: 1912 to order for R McCowen & Sons of Tralee, County Kerry, Ireland
Builders: Edwards & Co, Millwall, London
Grimsby Owners: Wynnefield Shipping Company 1915
Braunton Owners: G Clarke 1923
Bude Owners: WH Petherick and Sons 1937
Norwegian Owners: mid/late 1950s
Danish Owners: 1958 until 1991

Net registered tons: 70
Port of Registry: Barnstaple

Steel built with 80hp semi-diesel engine and hinged bowspit 1912

Irish Sea trades of bricks, coal, oats, timber and similar from 1912
Bridgewater to Liverpool brick trade from 1915
Southwest coastal trades from 1923
Mainly coal from Lydney, Gloucestershire and South Wales ports into Bude from 1937
New engine by Crossley Bros Ltd of Manchester, fitted 1946
General trade in Baltic from 1958 to 1977, when named *Karna*
Sandsucker, 1977 to 1984, Remmenstrand, as *Ral*
Gravel and sand dredger, Remmestrand, Jutland Peninsular from 1977 to 1991, as *Ral*

29. The *Traly*, her key dates, owners, registration and main trade

The closeness of the links between the sea-faring communities of Britain, Ireland, Scandinavia and the Continent of Europe as well as North America, is demonstrated not only by the trade and trading routes of the Westcountry ketches but also by where they were built and where they ended their days. Both the *Dido C* and the *Traly*, two ketches built in the twentieth century, provide instances of this interconnectedness. The 1921 built *Dido C* was built in Scandinavia for the Baltic trade and, having carried, in the main, coal from Lydney to the Westcountry ports and down to the Isles of Scilly, ended her days at Kircubbin, Northern Ireland in 1964. And the *Traly*, built in 1912 for the Irish Sea trade, moved onto the coastal trade of South West Britain and finally, following nearly forty years of work around the Baltic Sea, ended her days on the Jutland Peninsular in 1991.

The *Traly* first truly came to the notice of the Westcountry ketch watchers when she was purchased from her Braunton owners in 1937 by the Bude family of merchants and master mariners, the Pethericks. The *Traly* was purchased as the replacement for the Petherick's well-known 125 year old ketch the *Ceres*, which had foundered off Baggy Point in 1936 with a cargo of slag. The *Ceres*, at the time of her loss, had been the last ketch trading into Bude, and her replacement was welcomed with relief, enthusiasm and joy by the whole community there. Illustration 30 shows people crowding to watch the *Traly* being carefully guided into the Bude Canal for the first time.

For close on twenty years the *Traly* traded from Bude. This trade was mainly with coal, from Lydney and the Cardiff Bay ports into Bude for both domestic use and the gas works. Her outward bound cargoes were often of grain. But her trade, in common with the other ketches still working, was diminishing. In the mid 1950s her then captain, Oswald Jeffery sustained a serious on-board injury. The *Traly* traded under an Appledore

30. The *Traly* being welcomed into Bude, April 1937

captain, WH Hocking, for about two more years before being sold by the Pethericks in 1958 to Captain NH Ammersboll of Copenhagen. The *Traly* last entered the Bude Canal in the June of 1956, with 120 tons of flour from Avonmouth and left with 140 tons of wheat for Swansea. The *Traly* left Appledore for the last time on May 2nd 1958 to load coal at Swansea before leaving for the Baltic and her next forty years of work, first of all as the *Karna* and latterly as the *Ral*.

31. The *Traly* moored at Bude for the first time, April 1937

32. The *Traly* at Rolle Quay, Barnstaple,
barbed wire war defences in evidence, 1939

The following photograph is of the *Traly* with the hobblers alongside about to be guided into the Bude Canal to unload and load at the quay. The hobblers were the men who used warping ropes to guide the vessels into the non-tidal canal basin at the correct point of the tide by getting a purchase on the warping posts positioned along the high tide channel. Many associated trades and activities went for ever with the demise of the trading ketches and the *Traly* was the very last ketch to trade for a living out of Bude.

33. The *Traly*, the hobblers alongside, at Bude, 1946

The adjacent picture, illustration 34, is of the *Traly*, waiting for the tide to sail from Avonmouth's Royal Edward Dock in 1954. Moored alongside her in this picture are two River Severn motor barges, *River King* and *Sunrisen*. Dwarfing all three small vessels is the Liverpool registered Harrison Line cargo liner *Astronomer*. Robert Shopland recalls during the 1950s regularly seeing the *Traly*, sometimes under sail, but usually

34. The *Traly*, waiting for the tide, Royal Edward Dock, Avonmouth, 1954

making her smoky diesel passage along the Bristol Channel to and from Avonmouth, carrying grain and animal feeding stuffs.

The life of the *Traly* demonstrates a particular experience of role change shared by quite a number of these small craft in that, over the years, she metamorphosed from an elegant yacht-like trading vessel often under sail, into an engine-only, longer and sturdier, workhorse. In the case of the *Traly* she became a sand and gravel dredger working the Norwegian fjords. Robert Shopland's 1991 article, published in *Ships Monthly* following the demise of the *Traly*, records this change over time experienced by the *Traly* most tellingly. Starting life as one of the last trading ketches to be built in Britain she was

35. The *Traly* moored at Swansea, 1951

also probably the first vessel of her type to be completed with an auxiliary engine, rather than having it added later. As a motor ketch, the *Traly* did not carry a main top-mast and her bowspit was hinged, this latter being a feature of the Thames barges. The *Traly*, of course, was built at Millwall, London. Latterly, this bowspit was removed. She worked mainly under power, sometimes setting a Bermudan-style mainsail should the wind be favourable.

36. The *Traly*, 1970, after lengthening, but still with original foremast, now a sand-sucker

37. The *Traly*, 1984, at Remmanstrand, by then a sand-dredger

38. The *Traly*, 1991, at Remmanstrand,
after eighty years of work before being broken up

The following photograph, a favourite of mine, is of a much younger *Traly*, taken in 1955 from the *Agnes*, while both vessels were under sail heading towards Bull Point Lighthouse, North Devon. The ketches were much loved and much appreciated by those who sailed and worked them, and this picture appears to me to capture both the pleasure and the rivalry enjoyed during the life and times of these small vessels.

39. The *Traly* heading towards Bull Point Lighthouse,
taken from the *Agnes*, 1955

Endpiece

Within Billie Mitchell's personal collection of photographs and papers, mainly about the *Agnes* but also about other Westcountry ketches as well, this colour photograph of the Westcountry ketch, the *Mary Eliezer*, to my delight, surfaced.

The life and times of the *Mary Eliezer*, as with other ketches surviving into the late twentieth and early twenty-first centuries, share bits and pieces of maritime history with all three ketches of this small book. For instance, the *Mary Eliezer* was built at the beginning of the twentieth century in 1904: the *Traly* was built in 1912. Both were steel built. She experienced friendly fire, as was the case with the *Agnes*, while at anchor off Portland in 1932. The torpedo that struck the *Mary Eliezer* went on to hit a coal hulk moored beyond her, while the bolt that hit the *Agnes* tangled in the rigging and fell to the deck. The two trainee boys on board the *Mary Eliezer* at the time the torpedo struck plugged the hole made by the torpedo with a mattress to prevent water coming in. The *Mary Eliezer* was later repaired by the Admiralty. Her cargoes were grain to Swansea and slag back to Barnstaple and Bideford, as well as coal. She regularly did the quite lengthy round trip with coal between Southampton and the Westcountry.

Like the *Clara May*, the *Mary Eliezer*, was owned for a time by one of the Braunton syndicates, which included members of the Braunton family of mariners, the Clarkes, from around 1920 until 1947. She was sold in 1947 to Danish owners, as was the *Traly* in the late fifties. This was following the post-war government decision to support road transport over and above waterway and coastal transport in Britain. And, like both the *Agnes* and *Traly* she did have name changes, (ketch name changes were relatively common), first to the *Stenbidden* or *Stonefisher* and then reverting to the *Mary Eliezer* once more. She was used as a store ship by the Royal Navy 1939 -1945.

64

40. The ketch *Mary Eliezer*, built 1904, moored at Valletta, Malta on 14th January 1998

As with all the ketches, the *Mary Eliezer,* ninety-four years old at the time of her 1998 photograph, would easily be able to contribute to a whole small social history of her own. Here she serves to provide a summary with which to conclude.

Acknowledgments

My thanks go to the following individuals:-

Ray Harris, for his detailed, written account of his recollections of life on board the *Clara May* and the Malta encounter

Billie Mitchell, for access to and use of his personal collection of *Agnes* memorabilia and photographs, as well as the one-to-one conversations about his fifteen years as crew to his father on board the *Agnes*

Robert Shopland, Editor of *Ships Monthly* 1974 to 2000, for his detailed correspondence about and photographs of the *Traly* and other ketches

Andrew Byrom, personal maritime photographic archive

Anne Longley, Tregaskes family member, family papers and photographs of the *Agnes*

Maurice Batley, the North Devon and Canada timber trade and shipbuilding connection

George and Ann Wells the North Devon and Canada timber trade and shipbuilding connection

David Jenkins, National Waterfront Museum, Swansea, for the Spillers Flour Mills detail

Pat Wiggett, North Devon Museum Trust, Appledore

Jackie Edwards, Braunton Museum, Braunton

Michael Pryce-Jones, for the author photograph on the back cover illustration

My thanks go also to the following institutions:-

The North Devon Museum Trust at Appledore, (the Edwin Blight Collection of annotated maritime photographs; the Margaret Pollock Collection of maritime newspaper cuttings 1947 to 1980) Braunton Museum, North Devon; Bude-Stratton Museum, Cornwall

The National Waterfront Museum, Swansea; The National Museum of Wales, Cardiff
The Mitchell Library, Glasgow
Northam Branch Library, Northam, North Devon

Articles consulted

1952: Philip Kershaw, 'William Ashburner's Fate', in *Sea Breezes,* Vol XIV, P.294-295

1955: Philip Kershaw, 'Bristol Channel Changes', in *Sea Breezes*, Vol XX, P.68-69

1957: Philip Kershaw, 'Sail Review', in *Sea Breezes*, Vol 24, P.11-13

1991: Robert Shopland, 'Tribute to Traly', in *Ships Monthly*, August 1991, P.41

2004: PAB Thomas, 'Braunton: Home of the Last Fleet of Sailing Coasters', in *The Mariner's Mirror,* P.290-304

Books consulted

1970: A & M Langham: *Lundy,* David and Charles

1970: Grahame Farr: *Ships and Harbours of the Exmoor Coast*, The Exmoor Press

1971: Clive Carter: *The Blizzard of '91*, David & Charles

1974: Basil Greenhill & W. J. Slade: *West Country Coasting Ketches*, Conway Maritime Press

1977: Rennie Bere: *The Story of Budehaven*, Bude-Stratton Town Council

1980: Samuel E Ellacott: *Braunton Ships and Seamen*, Quest (Western) Publications

1986: Gordon Mote: *The Westcountrymen*, Badger Books

2003: Basil Greenhill & Ann Giffard: *Westcountrymen in Prince Edward's Isle*, Formac Publishing, Nova Scotia, 3rd Edition

2003: David Cordingly: *Billie Ruffian: The 'Bellerophon' and the Defeat of Napoleon*, Bloomsbury

2004: Giles Milton: *White Gold*, Hodder & Stoughton